The Ancient EGYPTIANS

Revised and Updated

JANE SHUTER

Heinemann Library
Chicago, Illinois

Customer Service 888-454-2279
Visit our website at www.heinemannraintree.com

Designed by Richard Parker and Q2A Solutions
Printed in China by WKT Company Ltd

11 10 09 08 07
10 9 8 7 6 5 4 3 2 1

New edition ISBNs: 13 digit ISBNs:
1-403-48810-X (hardback)   978-1-403-48810-7 (hardback)
1-403-48817-7 (paperback)   978-1-403-48817-6 (paperback)

The Library of Congress has cataloged the first edition of this book as follows:
Shuter, Jane.
   The ancient Egyptians / Jane Shuter.
   p.   cm. — (History opens windows)
   Includes index.
   Summary: Describes life in ancient Egypt, including farming, religion, government, and medicine.
   ISBN 0-431-05705-2 (lib. bdg.)
   1. Egypt—Civilization—To 332 B.C.—Juvenile literature.
   [1. Egypt—Civilization—To 332 B.C.]   I. Title. II. Series.
   DT61.S65   1997
   932—DC21
                        96-53256
                          AC

Acknowledgments
The publishers would like to thank the following for permission to reproduce photographs:
Alamy, p. **29**; Bridgeman Art Library/British Museum, London p. **30**; British Museum. pp. **7**, **8**, **12**, **16**, **17**, **19**, **22**, **25**, **27**; Robert Harding Picture Library, p. **2**; Michael Holford, p. **21**; Wellcome Institute Library, p. **28**; Hulton Picture Company, p. **29** (bottom).

Cover photograph reproduced with permission of The Art Archive / Dagli Orti.

Every effort has been made to contact copyright holders of any material reproduced in this book. Any omissions will be rectified in subsequent printings if notice is given to the publisher.

Contents

Some words are shown in bold, **like this**.
You can find out what they mean by looking in the glossary.

Introduction

Most of Egypt is a desert of sand and rocks. The Nile River runs through it from south to north. People who came to Egypt usually lived beside the river, because it was the only place where crops could grow.

2650 BC: step pyramid

2566 BC: Great pyramid

2400 BC: end of pyramid building

2040 BC

2686 BC

2184 BC

1782 BC

1570 BC

EARLY PERIOD

OLD KINGDOM

MIDDLE KINGDOM

3000 BC

2000 BC

There were people living in Egypt more than 5,000 years ago. People lived in small villages. Settlers came from the west, south, east, and northeast. They liked the valley of the Nile River, because they could catch fish and grow many types of crops there.

Ancient Egyptian **civilization** began around 3000 BC. This was when a king, called a **pharaoh**, began to rule the whole country. We divide Egyptian civilization into four periods. We call them the Early Period, the Old Kingdom, the Middle Kingdom, and the New Kingdom. You can see these periods marked on the timeline below. In between, there were wars. The pharaohs stopped ruling when the **Romans** took control in 30 BC.

The Nile River

The ancient Egyptians invented the shadoof, shown here, to lift water from the Nile River. Shadoofs are still used today.

The Nile River floods every year. As the water recedes, it leaves behind rich soil. The land that has been flooded is the only place where crops can grow.

The Egyptians wanted to grow more crops. But to do this they needed more water. They had to keep some of the flood water from draining back into the river. This would allow them to make more fields. They also had to find a way to get water from the river all year.

The Egyptians saw that the flood water could be held back with ponds and canals. Then they could use the water. It was hard work to dig the ponds and canals. The Egyptians had to clear and repair them all the time. They could only do this if they all worked together.

The Egyptians got more than water from the Nile. Here we see a nobleman hunting river birds to eat. The people also ate fish and used reeds to make baskets and boats.

Farming

The Egyptians farmed the land when the flood waters of the Nile River receded. They had to grow crops that could be harvested before the next flood. The most important crops were wheat and barley, which were used to make bread and beer. These were what most Egyptians ate and drank.

Another important crop was **flax**, used to make cloth. The Egyptians also grew fruit and vegetables. They ate a lot of onions, garlic, dates, and grapes.

The ancient Egyptians grew grapes to eat and to make wine.

Farmers used animals to help them do the hard work in the fields.

The Egyptians kept geese for their eggs and cows for their milk. They also hunted river birds and fish. They had no farm machines. Goats and sheep pressed the seed into the ground with their feet as soon as it was planted. An ox pulled the plow, and trampled the grain to get the **husks** off.

The Pharaoh

The Egyptians had to work together to control the Nile River. This was the best way to grow plenty of food, so that everyone had enough to eat. People often work together better if there is someone in charge. This person can make sure that all the work is done at the right time. In Egypt this person was called the **pharaoh**. He was seen as more like a god than just a person.

Tutankhamen is the most famous of the pharaohs. He was only about eight years old when he became pharaoh. He is famous because his people hid his tomb so well that it is the only tomb of a pharaoh that has not been robbed. The tomb was found in 1922, full of treasures such as the **sarcophagus** shown here.

Pharaoh Tutankhamen's sarcophagus shows him holding signs for Upper and Lower Egypt. He has the goddesses of both regions on his crown. This is to show that he ruled all of Egypt.

Vulture, symbol of goddess of Upper Egypt

Cobra, symbol of goddess of Lower Egypt

Crook, symbol of Lower Egypt

Flail, symbol of Upper Egypt

How Egypt Was Ruled

The **scribes** were the only people who could write. This skill made them important, because they could keep track of all the food that was stored. Here a scribe is counting the geese.

On the opposite page is a picture that shows how the Egyptians divided up the work. The **pharaoh** was at the top, giving out the work. Under him were the **viziers**, high priests, and nobles. The Egyptians thought that all jobs were important except for those of the slaves, who were at the bottom. Slaves were mostly prisoners captured in battles.

Pharaoh   Queen

Nobles   Grand Viziers of Upper   High Priest and
                    and Lower Egypt   High Priestess

Governors

Craftworkers   Artists   Scribes   Tax Gatherers   Priests   Priestesses

Builders   Farmers   Scribes   Wab (common priests)

Slaves

Trade

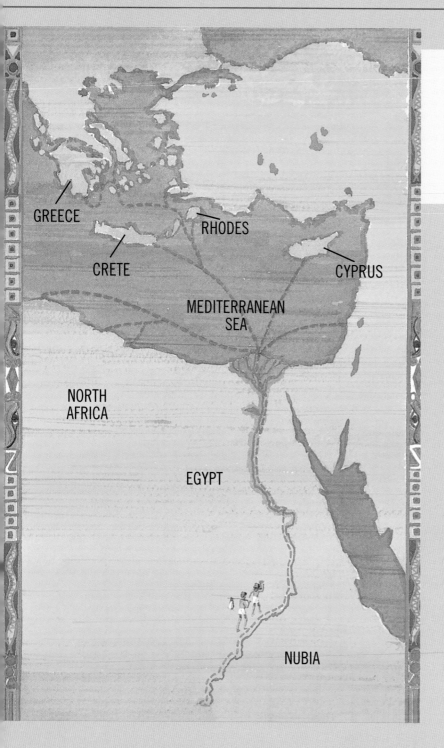

GREECE

RHODES

CRETE

CYPRUS

MEDITERRANEAN
SEA

NORTH
AFRICA

EGYPT

NUBIA

This map shows places with which the Egyptians traded.

The Egyptians did different jobs. Some were farmers and others were fishers. Some made shoes, while some brewed beer and made bread. They did not have money to buy these things from each other. Instead, they **traded** with each other to get the things that they wanted.

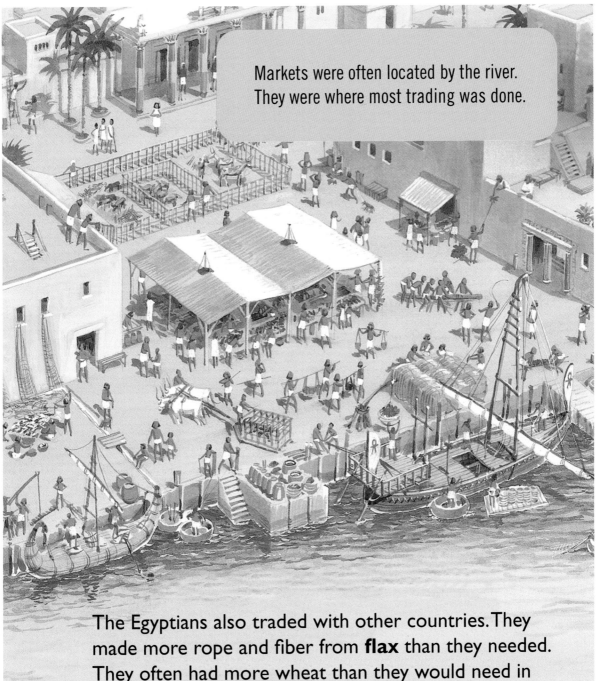

Markets were often located by the river. They were where most trading was done.

The Egyptians also traded with other countries. They made more rope and fiber from **flax** than they needed. They often had more wheat than they would need in the coming year. They traded their extra supplies for things that they did not have, such as wood, olive oil, silver, and gold. They traded with other countries in the Mediterranean, traveling mostly by boat.

Gods and Goddesses

The Egyptians had lots of gods. Some of the gods were known all over Egypt. Other gods were only known by people in a certain area. The Egyptians saw important things, such as the Sun or the Nile River, as gods. In pictures, they often showed their gods with animal heads.

Egyptians prayed to different gods at different times. If they thought that the Nile River was not going to flood, they prayed to the river goddess, Hapi. If a child was ill, they prayed to Bes, god of children, or Imhotep, god of medicine.

Hunefer

Anubis

Anubis

Ammut

Thoth

Every Egyptian house had its own **shrine**. This was a place where people could pray at any time.

The Egyptians also built huge **temples**. These were painted with pictures of stories about the gods. Each temple had a room where a statue of the god was kept. Only the priests were allowed to see it. Ordinary people were not allowed into the big temples. They left gifts outside for the gods.

The gods judge a dead man (Hunefer). They balance his heart against the feather of truth. If he has been good, he can go to the Fields of Iaru (Heaven). If he has been bad, Ammut eats him.

Hunefer

Horus

Osiris

Mummies

These Egyptian priests are oiling and wrapping a body.

The Egyptians thought that people who died went to a new world. They would need their bodies in the new world, so their bodies had to be kept from rotting. To do this, the Egyptians first removed the soft insides. They covered the body with a type of salt, to dry it out. They rubbed oils on it. Then they wrapped layers of cloth around it. A body that has been treated in this way is called a **mummy**.

They sometimes gave the mummy a face mask. It looked like the person did in real life. A rich person would have their jewels put on it. The mummy was put in a painted case called a **sarcophagus**. It was then buried in the ground or put in a tomb. Only some of the first **pharaohs** had **pyramids**. Most of them were buried in tombs cut in the rock in the Valley of the Kings.

A priestess in her sarcophagus, which shows what she looked like.

Pyramids

Pyramids were built out of big stone blocks. The blocks had to be dug up and cut to size. Then they had to be moved to the right place by sliding them along on wooden rollers. It took lots of men many years to build a pyramid.

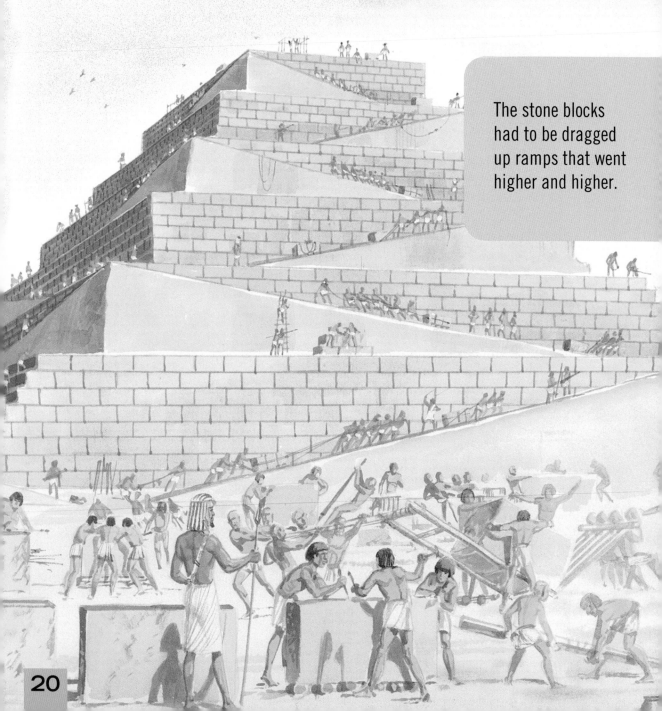

The stone blocks had to be dragged up ramps that went higher and higher.

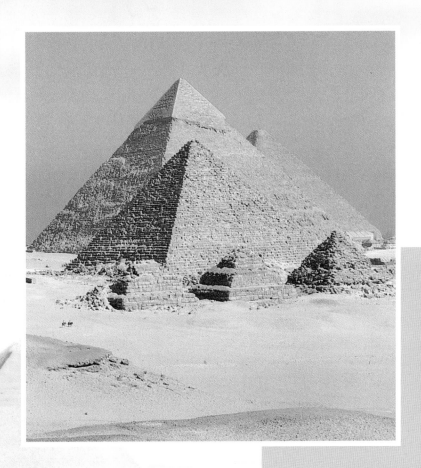

The Great Pyramid took 5,000 men 20 years to build. It is made from more than 2.3 million blocks of stone.

The **mummy** of the dead **pharaoh** was put into a small room in the middle of the pyramid. He had many things he might need for his next life. There were jewels, food, furniture, pots, and even model dolls to work for him. The entrances were closed, but the pyramids were often robbed, so the workers made secret rooms to bury the pharaohs in, with traps to catch the thieves.

Everyday Life

Egyptian life had a pattern. All the women worked in the home. Most Egyptian men worked at two jobs. When the water in the Nile was low, they worked on the land. When the Nile flooded, the men had other jobs. Some were builders or fishers. Others were artists or jewelers. Only the most important people and the priests did not farm.

Egyptians had very little furniture.

Egyptian clothes looked a lot like this. The big lumps on the women's heads are scented lumps of fat. They melted in the heat and ran down the women's faces. This kept them cool and made them smell nice.

It was very hot in Egypt, so people did not wear many clothes. Men, women, and children wore either thin cloth **kilts** or robes. Women wore as much makeup and jewelry as they could afford.

To stay cool, people shaved off all their hair. They wore wigs on special occasions.

Houses

The Egyptians built all houses in the same way. They used mud bricks for building. The walls were thick, to keep out the heat. The houses of important people had more rooms. They had lovely painted walls inside, but they looked the same on the outside.

Because it did not rain very often, there was no need to have sloping roofs to carry the rain away. The flat roofs were part of the house. People sat on their roofs. They dried their laundry by setting it on the roof. Most people cooked outside, so if they had no garden they did their cooking on the roof.

Inside an Egyptian craftworker's house

Vent

Awning

Earth floor

The houses had rooms under the ground. These rooms were dark and cool. They were very good for storing food and drink.

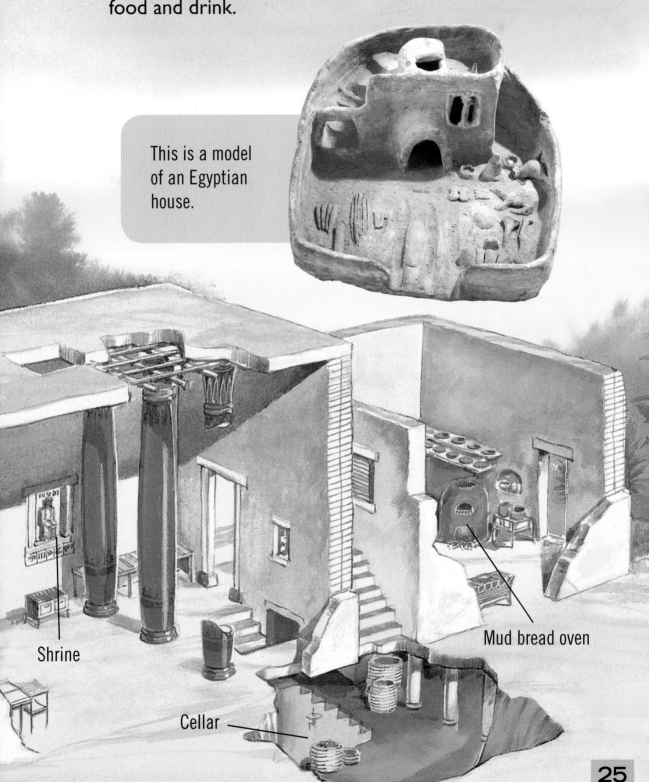

This is a model of an Egyptian house.

Shrine

Mud bread oven

Cellar

Children

Children in Egypt grew up to do the same jobs as their parents. Girls stayed at home with their mothers. They learned how to take care of the house, bake bread, and weave **flax**. Boys went to work with their fathers and helped as much as they could. They only went to school if they were going to work as a **scribe**.

Egyptian children worked hard.

Here are some Egyptian children's toys. They are made from wood and reeds.

Very young children stayed at home with their mothers. Many of their games were like games today. They played racing games, tag, and leapfrog. They had balls and wooden toys. Older children played a game like chess, called senet.

Medicine

An Egyptian doctor had many tools.

Making **mummies** helped the Egyptians learn how the body worked. They saw the lungs, heart, and other organs when they took them out of the body. This helped them discover better ways to treat sick people.

The Egyptians tried to make people healthy in different ways. They made medicines from plants. They treated snake bites by sucking the poison from the wound. They tried to keep clean. Everyone tried to wash their clothes and dishes often.

Egyptians carried magic charms with them to keep illness and evil away.

The Egyptians also believed in magic. They thought that evil **spirits** made people ill. They prayed to a god to make the spirits go away. They drank magic drinks to make them well. They wore magic charms to keep evil spirits away.

The magic potion recipe above calls for beetles and a snake's head.

End of the Empire

Egypt became part of the Greek **empire** in 332 BC. This changed the way people in Egypt lived. Three hundred years later the **Romans** took control of Egypt. Slowly, the Egyptians gave up their special way of life and the **pharaohs** stopped ruling. This was the end of the ancient Egyptian **civilization**.

This is an Egyptian mummy case but the painting of the face is a Roman painting. The two cultures mixed when the Romans took control of Egypt.

Glossary

civilization way of life of a group of people

empire group of territories or lands controlled by one country

flax plant that can be made into cloth

husk hard outer covering of a grain such as wheat

kilt type of skirt worn by men or women

mummy dead body that has been specially treated and wrapped in cloth so that it does not rot

pharaoh ruler of an ancient Egyptian kingdom

pyramid structure that has a square base and sloping triangular sides that meet at the top

Romans people of the ancient Roman Empire (500 BC–AD 476)

sarcophagus painted case in which a mummy was stored

scribe person whose job it was to read, write, and keep records

shrine special place for worshiping a god or gods

spirits magical beings or forces that we cannot see

temple building for religious worship

trade to swap one type of item for another instead of buying and selling using money

viziers men who worked for the pharaoh and had a lot of power

Find Out More

Books to read
Fix, Alexandra. *History and Activities of Ancient Egypt: Hands-On Ancient History.* Chicago: Heinemann Library, 2006.
Shuter, Jane. *Life Along the River Nile: Picture the Past.* Chicago: Heinemann Library, 2004.

Using the Internet
Explore the Internet to find out more about the ancient Egyptians. Use a search engine, such as www.yahooligans.com or www.internet4kids.com and type in a keyword or phrase such as "Tutankhamen" or "pyramids."

Index